CW00419064

A PASSION FOR
lingerie

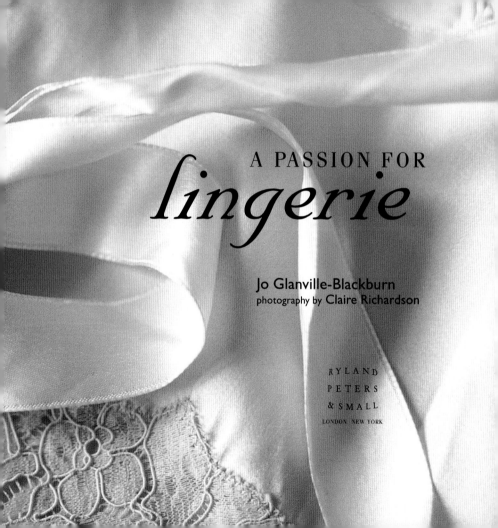

A PASSION FOR
lingerie

Jo Glanville-Blackburn
photography by **Claire Richardson**

RYLAND
PETERS
& SMALL
LONDON NEW YORK

Designer Pamela Daniels
Editor Miriam Hyslop
Location Researcher Tracy Ogino
Production Gemma Moules
Art Director Gabriella Le Grazie
Publishing Director Alison Starling
Stylist Twig Hutchinson

First published in Great Britain
in 2005 by Ryland Peters & Small
20–21 Jockey's Fields
London WC1R 4BW
www.rylandpeters.com

10 9 8 7 6 5 4 3 2 1
Printed in China

ISBN 1 84172 975 2
A CIP record for this book is
available from the British Library.

contents

introduction

If you're wearing lingerie that makes you feel glamorous, you're already halfway to turning heads.

Beautiful, sensual underwear is an extension of your body and your sense of style. It epitomizes the very art of personal care and dressing. Lingerie offers a unique glimpse into your secret self. On the surface, a woman may appear neat, cool, calm and collected, but catch a glimpse of stocking top, a hint of turquoise lace and tulle or a sensual rustle of vibrant silk and her persona may be changed irrevocably. And when you wear fabulous satins and silks next to your skin you simply exude confidence and allure. It makes you focus on your body. You feel sensual. So wear lingerie for you, to feel good about your self.

For centuries, the outline of women's bodies has been shaped, controlled and moulded by lingerie, corsetry and petticoats. So isn't it amazing how, since the body has been freed from the restrictions of these body-sculpting garments, women should choose to impose their own restrictions, by having so-called 'figure faults' corrected by cosmetic surgery?

16

It was the Victorians who first embraced the French term 'lingerie' to describe our undergarments.

From the 1920s, women endured breast reductions so they could wear the boyish fashions. By the end of the 1930s the breast was back in vogue, so the first surgical enlargements were carried out (though unspeakably awful when compared with modern procedures). Today, whether by drastic diets, obsessive body training or groundbreaking surgery, the silhouette is being manipulated further. People with ordinary lives and modest incomes view body-enhancing and sculpting surgery as their right to satisfy emotional needs and fashion ideals.

*Women have
two types of
underwear.
One black, tiny,
and the size of a
micro dot;
the other, grey
and the size of
Buckinghamshire*

JO BRAND,
UK COMEDIENNE

The ideal solution to figure-slimming is not to squash it all into a girdle as our mothers and grandmothers did. Surely we've advanced further than this? Tummy control pants may hold you in better, but they certainly won't make you feel any better about your body and yourself.

The body is under government scrutiny. Health and fitness is the twenty-first century dogma. Exercise reduces physical and psychological body problems and, ultimately, you will get a better body – one that looks and feels better for life.

I believe that today, more than ever, women need to be more in touch with their bodies. Body confidence is at an all-time low. Doing something about it is at an all-time high. By wearing beautiful lingerie next to your skin and investing in exquisite pieces that feel fabulous, you will feel more fabulous about yourself, too. Consider lingerie a treat for your body that goes beyond retail therapy. Lingerie is psychologically good for you. It's time to be inspired...

vintage

boudoir

When you think 'vintage' lingerie, put aside thoughts of 'worn' and think 'boudoir' instead. These exquisite pieces can be worn momentarily, for the bedroom alone but not for you alone...

Fashion consistently repeats itself, ensuring that exquisite fabrics, antique lace and delicate stitching will have a place in our hearts, as well as in the top drawer, forever. Inspired by everything from elaborate Victorian lacing and corsetry to elegant 1920s chiffon-bow-and-tie details, vintage style is an eclectic mix of 'fashion pieces' that makes the wearing of lingerie a very special experience.

divine inspiration

Today's resurgence in fashion for all things bedecked with ribbons and bows, has hip lingerie designers, such as Damaris Evans, FrostFrench (design duo Sadie Frost and Jemima French) and Sarah Pask turning to vintage details for their divine inspiration.

From deep, plunging, cheeky silk tulle knickers, and ruched, tutu ballet-style pants, to Victoriana satin, silk and chiffon camisoles, more and more women are choosing gorgeous underwear as one of life's little luxuries. Whereas previously lingerie was perceived as something to entertain partners, women are now finally learning to enjoy the fashion of lingerie for themselves.

Q: *Panties, knickers, briefs, pants . . . what should the modern woman call her underwear?*

A: *Never panties — that's for a six year-old in the US. Only ever knickers!*

underwear as outerwear

If you're a genuine vintage fan, then you'll know that a 1940s or 1950s size 6 is more like today's UK 8 or even 10.

As fashion embraces a more eclectic sense of style, self-expression through merging vintage and modern, lingerie is now as much about outerwear as underwear. With such exquisite details as beading, gemstones, ribbons, sequins and bows, why hide it?

The art of layering is all about style. Just because bras are worn underneath our clothes, the very cut, fit and style of lingerie today has evolved to such an extent that lingerie is too pretty to cover up, and can now be as much a part of your outfit as you want it to be. Sheer, diaphanous chiffon requires the prettiest bra or camisole to peep through, corsets and basques are an item all on their own, while ribbons and lace simply beg to be seen.

Vintage lingerie – from intricate embroidery and prints to lace and beads – looks so good on, it just has to be put on show. So, undo that extra button, slip on a contrasting sheer chiffon slip of a dress, attach a corsage, and you've got the look.

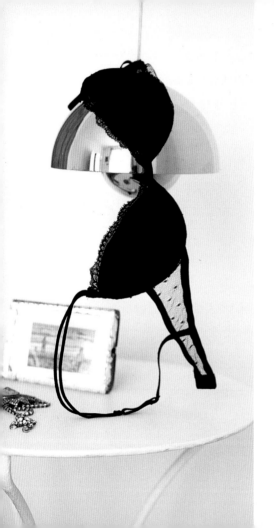

what is sexy?

Nothing, save your perfume, gets as close to your skin on such a regular basis as your lingerie. Interpretations of just what makes underwear sexy varies from woman to woman, and from man to man.

'The sexiest part of lingerie is the way it makes you feel,' says Jacqueline Gold, CEO of lingerie stores Ann Summers and Knickerbox. 'If you feel sensual and confident, then you feel sexy and seductive. The specific cut of lingerie and the way it feels on your skin are as important as the colour and style.'

get inventive

Nothing else that we wear has such an effect on the psyche. So choose lingerie either to enhance or simply to show off what you've got.

There is a boundary to men's passions when they act from feelings; but none when they are under the influence of imagination.

EDMUND BURKE

When choosing new sexy lingerie, banish any negative thoughts you may have about whether or not you'll look good in it. Sexy lingerie comes in many different sizes and guises, all designed to make you look your best – including hiding your flaws and accentuating your assets. The secret is finding the right kind of sexy lingerie for you.

Concentrate on the parts of your body that you're most comfortable with and choose lingerie to emphasize them. Got great legs? Choose something short – a babydoll or chemise. Prefer to hide wide hips? Choose something with a fuller skirt. If you're tall you'll suit a long gown, but if you're petite a beautiful lingerie set may be more flattering.

I would never, ever, ever design a crotchless knicker. That is one piece of lingerie that isn't humorous. It leaves nothing to the imagination, and has no wit.

DAMARIS EVANS, LINGERIE DESIGNER

SURE BET A slippery silk robe. Underneath, you can wear something equally beautiful or – ta-da! – nothing at all.

SURE BET Texture is everything – if it feels soft to the touch, it will be sexy to wear and to caress.

MYSTERY Keep it covered. It's generally agreed by men that it's what you can't see, rather than what you can, that makes lingerie so sexy. Case in point: the stocking top – men crave the tantalizing glimpse of bare flesh at the stocking top.

AVOID Anything flannel. This is seduction, not sleep, you're after.

AVOID Lingerie that looks uncomfortable to wear, or tricky to remove, such as a corset. It could ruin the moment.

visible panty line

Damaris Evans, provocative designer for Jade Jagger,
Kirsten Dunst, Courtney Love, Liberty Ross and Liv Tyler,
was at a party with an actress friend who was 'Wearing a
black pencil skirt, no tights and very special high heels'.
It was very clear to see that she had a zigzag knicker line.
When asked if she was wearing a pair of corset knickers, she
said she was, then added: 'Oops, I'd better take my skirt off
then.' Wonderful priorites.

the ultimate seduction

It's the slipperiness of silk, the sauciness of satin and the delicate fingering of lace that can make lingerie so arousing.

It's the temptation, the suggestion, the promise of passion to come, held suspended in the balance. Seduction is all this and more. It's the pleasing of the senses. Lingerie undoubtedly pleases the eye – the lure of a heavenly body wrapped in beautiful fabric, like wrapping paper, tied with ribbons, promising a treat in store. Your touch – the soft intimate caress, creamy soft skin and undulating curves. A kiss – your soft breath like a gentle whisper. Your scent – like a fine veil over your skin, captivating his heart as you lean closer.

Whatever your seductive style – the innocent ingénue draped in ivory satin or the divine temptress encased in black lace – choose lingerie and accessories that you feel confident and comfortable in. Ultimately, you will project your sensuality simply by revealing the seductive pieces of lingerie of your own choice. Make it your own fantasy, your own piece of heaven. Above all, make it you. Buying to please another seldom leaves you pleased with yourself.

S C

body-
ulpting

the corset

This most unique piece of lingerie,
originally designed to enhance and mould
the female form, has been revived and
redesigned over the centuries. The
corset is now something of a fashion
icon. Its disappearance and
reappearance throughout twentieth-
century fashion reflects the cyclical
changing of female shapes. Today it is a
garment no longer designed for
constraint, but for style, worn much as
any other top – perhaps underneath a
chic jacket or even with jeans.

Still, the allure of the corset remains.
It offers the promise of a gift – a present
bound up tightly, and the enticement of
the delicate ribbon that, once unravelled,
reveals all its delightful contents.

Corsetry was the original figure-training for teenage girls, often so tightly laced that girls fainted.

We have the Victorians to thank for the corset. For velvet and lace trimmings, ribbons to tug, row upon row of tiny covered buttons slightly undone. The age of innocence? We should give the Victorians more credit.

Throughout the twentieth century, the corset has evolved into bustiers, bodices and even armour, but it has left the indelible fantasy of an idealized, flattering tight-fitting female silhouette, which is timeless and still appeals today. It was British fashion designer Vivienne Westwood, who, in the mid-1970s, revived the use of the corset in its original form. Theatrical in style, Westwood established a new trend in the 1980s and 1990s, and inspired many more contemporary fashion designers such as Stella McCartney, Chloë, Thierry Mugler and Jean-Paul Gaultier to celebrate the beauty of women's bodies and design with wit, glamour and power.

retro

showing off our assets

Girls wear cotton, women wear lingerie.

From the picture-postcard naughtiness of the late 1940s to the pin-up girls of the 1950s, the postwar decades did us a huge favour – they taught us how to start showing off our assets. Fashion history has shown that in the 1950s, glamour was what women wanted most from life. They had been deprived during the war – making the desire for beauty and fashion all the more ubiquitous – and so, inspired by Hollywood's screen sirens such as Jayne Mansfield, Jane Russell and Marilyn Monroe, women demanded a new silhouette.

The first conical bra helped emulate the curves of glamorous film-star sweater girls, pushing breasts up and out. From this point on, lingerie history changed for the better. Bras were further revolutionized by the use of nylon, which made them better, lighter, prettier, more comfortable and easier to wash.

sweater-girl glamour

The classic retro shape of the 1950s was defined by an über-small waist, held in tight by a long-line girdle, while the breasts were encased in a heavily structured bra. Today, we still think of curves and a shapely silhouette when it comes to glamour. Stitched satin and waist-high pants help to hold a girl in place, and fit perfectly under dresses and evening wear.

Nowadays, modern figure-control fabric technology has created retro-inspired lightweight body-control pants, tights, all-in-one bodysuits and bras that give a smoother sihouette without ridges under clothes. The ultimate in utility fashion, these designs are intended solely to be worn, and never to be seen. Make that your fashion mantra.

In the past twenty years alone, waists and tummies have grown. And compared to our 1950s counterparts, the average British woman has gained 8 cm around the hips and 16 cm around the waist. But, thanks to the fun of Helen Fielding's character Bridget Jones, there's no shame to be had for wearing the occasional piece of body-firming underwear.

Marilyn Monroe deliberately had the stiletto heels of her shoes adjusted so that one heel was made slightly shorter than the other. This gave her body a deliberate sexy sway and sashay as she walked, helping to make her appear more vulnerable and so even sexier.

the right fit

Chances are you'll invest in every shape and shade of bra from your teens onwards. Throughout life, the body changes shape – either from diet, age or pregnancy – and the breasts are often the first place to show signs of distress. And it is highly likely that you will have many redundant bra styles and designs in your drawers – from sexy, alluring, comfy, sweater to cleavage styles, as well as the grey, frayed version that just 'always seems to fit best'.

You know it's a bad day when you put your bra on back to front and it fits better.

However, lingerie manufacturers say that up to 85 per cent of us walk around with a bra that doesn't fit. And guess what? A bra that doesn't fit does nothing for your figure. Without the right underwear, your clothes never look quite right. So, set aside a lingerie-clearing session, and throw out anything that doesn't do your figure justice.

Q: *Just how many items of lingerie does a woman really need?*
A: *Need is debatable, it's about enjoyment.*

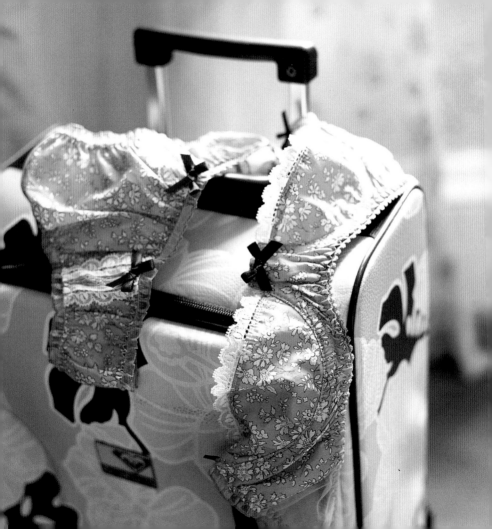

bra basics

The original Wonderbra was actually created in 1968. For many women the choice was between the bra or surgery. In the 1990s, when breast implants received bad press, the Wonderbra became even more popular.

∞ If you wear good-fitting bras, you should not be able to feel that you are wearing one at all.

∞ If the band at the back of the bra rides up the band of the bra is too big, so you need a smaller back size.

∞ If the under-wire is digging in under your armpit, your bra cup is too small. The under-wire should encase the breast, not dig into it.

∞ If the bra straps dig in, your bra is too big in the back and not big enough in the cup. This causes you to pull the straps up too tight for support.

∞ If your breasts are falling out of the bottom of the under-wire, the band of your bra is too big and the cup is too small.

∞ If your breasts overspill out of your bra, you need to increase your cup size, until you have a smoother silhouette under clothes.

romantic

romance

Fun and frivolous, dainty and adorable, flirty and cute – eternally youthful. When it comes to lingerie, romantics tend to prefer a rose-tinted, delicate pastel hue, which their seductive sisters might find too quaint. Crushed rosebuds, dainty sprigs, velvet embossing: prettiness personified. Romantic lingerie is always tantalizing, alluring and beguiling, but rarely risqué. French knickers, teddies, camisoles and tap pants – in precious silks that make you feel ladylike – are sophisticated yet chaste; charming, elegant and slightly sentimental.

Knickers have become like shoes... a girl can never have enough.

WILLIAM BAKER,
STYLIST AND
CO-DESIGNER
LOVE KYLIE

Just as innocently romantic is white cotton. Many men claim to prefer the simplicity and sporty appeal of white cotton to the frills and flounce of satin and silk. Of course, cotton has to be white – virginal white, pure. Think Calvin Klein: suddenly romantic equals modern too, not naive, just classic.

For classic romantic silk and lace, head to La Perla. This is the kind that makes you feel moneyed, even if you aren't. The Aston Martin of the lingerie world. Now, that's desirable.

something subtle

Forget the thong. Not every woman feels comfortable baring her bottom in a minuscule G-string and it's certainly not romantic. French knickers or hipster pants enhance your figure and leave an element of mystery that can be very alluring.

Choose depending on your level of ease with lingerie, there are many different styles and designs that will make you feel pretty and feminine, such as:

CHEMISE A straight gown that skims the body.

NEGLIGEE A loose, usually sheer, gown.

PEIGNOIR SET Negligee that includes a matching sheer robe.

BABYDOLL A short gown that fits around the bust, and flares towards the hemline – go pastel, not black.

BUSTIER A usually strapless elongated bra that provides extra lift to the breasts.

CAMISOLE A strappy top that can be paired with matching undies or worn under a jacket for work.

TEDDY A one-piece style, similar to a bodysuit.

TAP PANTS Soft, very short version of boxing shorts.

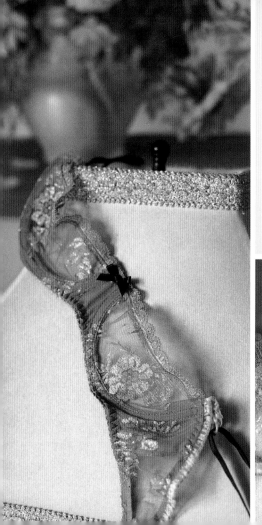

I can't imagine wearing nylon knickers — it's either white cotton knickers or special silk anything.

DAMARIS EVANS, LINGERIE DESIGNER

pretty in pink

Any colour so long as it's pink. Beyond a certain age, you don't want pink to be cute. A deep raspberry pink is more grown-up and sophisticated, whereas pale baby pink is just that – for the girls.

The fabric or material of your lingerie can also add a certain kind of attitude to your outfit. Body-clinging silks and slipper satins are tempting. What the eye can't see... Silk and chiffon are both smooth and romantic, while Lycra and spandex are tight-fitting and stretchy. Sheer material can express a certain innocent demeanour. The type of fabric or material you decide upon will only speak if you choose to let it. Find your own way of expressing how you feel with the lingerie, and don't be afraid to hide your conservative side for the night.

practically speaking

Lingerie, especially bras with under-wiring, is always best hand-washed with a mild soap detergent and lukewarm water. After rinsing, allow the garment to drain in the sink rather than wringing such fragile fabric. Then hang on a hanger (ideally plastic) and pin gently into place, so that it keeps its shape while it dries. Treated with care, your lingerie will last much longer. Iron out ribbon and bow details before storing. Any vintage-inspired items with special appliqué, such as camisoles or slips, may be better sent to the dry-cleaner's with experience in handling vintage or evening-wear clothing.

Keep a separate drawer or two for your lingerie. Ensure there are no sharp objects, emerging screws, etc. that may snag or pull on delicate silks and lace. Line the drawers with scented paper or add sachets of French lavender or rose to keep everything smelling sweet.

Silk has a magical quality of being able to hold the scent to your lingerie. Spritz a small silk square with your perfume, then drop it in to your lingerie drawer to leave it delicately scented.

ROJA DOVE,
PERFUMER

wedding

what to wear

Deciding what to wear underneath a wedding gown is often far more complicated than choosing the dress itself. Above all else, it's got to look good on the night. But it also has to work underneath your dress, be it silk, muslin, satin, chiffon, laced, corseted, scoop-necked or empire-lined.

One definitely to obey — always buy your bridal underwear once you've chosen your dress, and then wear it at every fitting.

Few of us may consider this vital until the last few days before the big day, yet what you wear underneath your dress makes or breaks how your wedding gown looks, falls and fits for the duration of the day – and just how comfortable you feel.

I would always advise two lingerie outfits: one for your wedding dress, which works with shaping your figure under the fabric so you look great and feel fabulous all day long; and then something pretty and fresh to slip into for your wedding night. Choose lingerie that's delicate, elegant and feminine. You might choose an ivory silk robe that looks sexy with something equally beautiful worn underneath. Or you may decide to wear nothing at all under the dress…

Remember: comfort is key on your wedding day. If you need to wear a bra underneath your dress, choose one that you can barely feel.

The garter was originally designed to hold up your hosiery on the day. The modern take on this dainty piece of lingerie is that it should be worn for good luck, so the groom can remove it at the end of the wedding reception and fling it to a mass of eager male guests. As for the bouquet, the lucky recipient of the garter is destined to be the next to marry.

Even under a long dress, tights or stockings should be worn, if only to protect your feet from rubbing in your 'virgin' wedding shoes – except, of course, on a beach. There's a wide range of hosiery available to brides, many with exquisite details on the ankles, or delicate lace and bows on top. One tip: stick to flesh-coloured hosiery, which is flattering and more subtle than pure white (which may simply look 'too much'). Keep a spare pair of stockings or tights to hand, for emergencies.

Guaranteed to be the most indulgent day of your life, make sure you pay close attention to what you wear under your gown and attempt to keep up the standard.

*What you wear underneath
your dress makes or breaks
how your wedding gown
looks, falls and fits for the
duration of the day.*

business credits

AUSTIQUE
330 King's Road
Chelsea
London SW3 5UR
t. 0870 3450800
www.austique.com

COCO DE MER
23 Monmouth Street
Covent Garden
London WC2H 9DD
t. 020 7836 8882
www.coco-de-mer.co.uk

DAMARIS
t. 020 8969 9866
www.damaris-london.com

EDA
132 King's Road
Chelsea
London SW3 4TR
t. 020 7584 0435
www.eda-lingerie.com

**ELLE MACPHERSON
INTIMATES**
t. 0800 236 366
www.ellemacpherson
intimates.co.nz

EMMA CASSI
Lace jewellery designer
www.emmacassi.com
t.020 8487 2836

FENWICK
t. 020 7629 9161l
www.fenwick.co.uk
Florence Torrens & Paul Frith
For details/bookings contact
paul@paulfrith.co.uk

JANET REGER
2 Beauchamp Place
London SW3 1NG
t. 020 7584 9386
www.janetreger.co.uk

**JOSEPHINE RYAN
ANTIQUES**
63 Abbeville Road
London SW4 9JW
t/f. 020 8675 3900
www.josephineryanantiques.co.uk

LIBERTY
Regent Street
London W1A 3BB
t. 020 7734 1234
www.liberty.co.uk

MAISONETTE
79 Chamberlayne Road
London NW10 3ND
Opening hours (Tues–Sat)
11.00–18.00
Contact Amanda Sellers
& Martin Barrell
t. 020 8964 8444
f. 020 8964 8464
www.maisonette.uk.com
maisonetteUK@aol.com

MARIANNE COTTERILL
The Lounge at Selfridges
t. 020 8931 6649
www.loungeonline.net

SPINA
12 Kingsgate Place
London NW6 4TA
t. 020 7328 5274
f. 020 7624 2078
www.spinadesign.co.uk
spinadesign@btconnect.com

picture credits

All photography by Claire Richardson

PAGES 29, 60 above right Emma Cassi's flat in London; designs by Emma Cassi.

PAGES 18, 26–27, 30–31, 36–37, 38, 44, 52, 56–57, 62 Marianne Cotterill's house in London – products available from The Lounge at Selfridges.

PAGES 12–13, 20–21, 24 Florence & Paul's Edwardian house in London.

PAGES 1, 14, 22, 48–49, 58 Josephine Ryan's house in London.

PAGE 41, 43, 53 Spina (tie-backs, tassels and crystal installations) private showroom – by appointment only.

PAGES 46–47 Amanda Sellers & Martin Barrell's flat in North West London.

acknowledgments

The author and publisher would like to thank the following writers, publishers and literary representatives for their permission to use copyright material: Vivienne Clore, on behalf of Jo Brand; Errin Mackness, at Halpern Associates, on behalf of Kylie Minogue and William Baker; Ghislain Pascal, on behalf of Jacqueline Gold of Ann Summers; Damaris Evans. With special thanks to Roja Dove, Harrods Haute Parfumerie and Shelly Vella.

My first bra was a B cup, at the tender age of 9½, and a very visible navy and white polka dot number. I've been obsessing ever since. Thanks Mum.